—African-American Biographies—

BARBARA JORDAN

Congresswoman, Lawyer, Educator

Series Consultant:
Dr. Russell L. Adams, Chairman
Department of Afro-American Studies, Howard University

Laura S. Jeffrey

Enslow Publishers, Inc.

44 Fadem Road	PO Box 38
Box 699	Aldershot
Springfield, NJ 07081	Hants GU12 6BP
USA	UK

Library of Congress Cataloging-in-Publication Data

Jeffrey, Laura S.
    Barbara Jordan: congresswoman, lawyer, educator / Laura S. Jeffrey.
        p. cm. — (African-American biographies)
    Includes bibliographical references (p.) and index.
    Summary: Explores the life and career of Barbara Jordan, from her
childhood in Houston, through her distinguished career in public office,
to her powerful influence as a speaker.
    ISBN 0-89490-692-5
    1. Jordan, Barbara, 1936–1996 —Juvenile literature. 2. Legislators—
United States—Biography—Juvenile literature. 3. Afro-American women
legislators—Biography—Juvenile literature. 4. United States. Congress.
House—Biography—Juvenile literature. 5. Women educators—United
States—Biography—Juvenile literature. [1. Jordan, Barbara, 1936–1996.
2. Legislators. 3. Afro-Americans—Biography. 4. Women—Biography.]
I. Title. II. Series.
E840.8.J62J45   1997
328.73'092—dc20
    [B]   96-19955
                                                              CIP
                                                               AC

Printed in the United States of America

10 9 8 7 6 5 4 3 2 1

Illustration Credits:
The Barbara Jordan Archives, Texas Southern University, pp. 4, 21, 28,
40, 43, 45, 51, 58, 60, 69, 71, 73, 76, 80, 92, 94.

Cover Illustration:
Lyndon B. Johnson School of Public Affairs, University of Texas

CONTENTS

Barbara Jordan

1

A POWERFUL VOICE

warm and sunny day was predicted for Washington, D.C., on August 8, 1994, when eight men and women gathered at the White House. The group had come together because President Bill Clinton wanted to honor these Americans for their years of public service.

In a short ceremony recorded by news reporters and photographers, Clinton presented each of the men and women with the Presidential Medal of Freedom. This award, which was established in 1963, is very prestigious. It is given to Americans who have shown exceptional achievement in national security, world peace, culture, or other public service.

One of the 1994 recipients was Barbara Charline Jordan. This African-American woman had compiled an impressive public-service record during the past thirty years. In the 1960s, she became the first African-American woman elected to the Texas State Senate. Then, in the 1970s, Jordan became the first African-American woman from the South elected to the United States Congress. She retired from public office in 1978 but continued to serve and speak out for the American people. At Clinton's request, Jordan led a commission on immigration reform. She served as ethics adviser to Texas governor Ann Richards. She also was involved with several other civic projects.

On the day Jordan received the medal from President Clinton, she sat in a wheelchair. Jordan could not walk because she had multiple sclerosis, which is a disease of the central nervous system. Her voice, however, remained strong and commanding. Messages she delivered in the unforgettably deep, resonating tones of her voice made her an enduring American political hero.

"I am very excited to be a recipient [of the Medal of Freedom]," Jordan told a reporter a week before the ceremony. "It's an extraordinary honor, and I am delighted."[1]

Jordan's words were simple yet powerful, just as they had been throughout her career. Sometimes, however, her words also were controversial.

"Throw away your crutches and quit complaining because you are black," she said in a speech to the National Association for the Advancement of Colored People (NAACP) when she was a state senator. "Don't belch, choke, smoke, and wish for something to go away. Because when you are finished belching, choking, smoking and wishing, society will still be here."[2]

Other times, Jordan's words united a divided nation. When she was a United States congresswoman in the 1970s, she gave a moving speech explaining why she would vote to impeach President Richard Nixon over the Watergate scandal. In June 1972, burglars linked to key members of Nixon's staff had broken into the headquarters of the Democratic National Committee in Washington, D.C. Subpoenaed White House conversations, which Nixon had secretly tape-recorded for his own use, proved the president was aware of the illegal activities.

In her speech, Jordan said that no one, not even the president, could disregard the United States Constitution. "My faith in the Constitution is whole, it is complete, it is total," she articulated forcefully. The speech, which was televised, helped restore public confidence in elected leaders and turned Jordan into a folk hero.[3]

Jordan's words also were inspiring. As keynote speaker on the opening night of the 1992 Democratic National Convention, she stirred the crowd with her call for change.

"Why not change from a party with a reputation of tax and spend to one with a reputation of investment and growth?" she asked. "Change. Change. A growth economy is a must."[4]

"On the toughest night of the week, Ms. Jordan gave what surely must be one of the most remarkable speeches delivered at a recent Democratic convention," Daniel Henninger wrote in *The Wall Street Journal.* "When she began to talk, the hall quieted, and save for the applause, it stayed quiet."[5]

Jordan's words were motivating as well. She had this to say in the fall of 1993, when she helped establish the Character Counts Coalition to teach young people strong moral values:

> If we are successful, we are going to make character the Number One call of young people in this country. They are going to think before they act because they know that if they do the wrong thing, that there are consequences, and they may not like these consequences. Kids must now understand that they are responsible for their actions . . . [and adults] are responsible for making sure that young people know what is expected of them.[6]

Jordan herself learned responsibility at a young age. Her strict but loving parents made it clear that Barbara and her two sisters were never to use their race or humble beginnings as excuses for failure.

So despite a lack of money, despite growing up in the segregated South, Barbara Jordan persevered. She excelled in high school—even though she sometimes got into trouble for talking too much. In law school, Jordan often stayed up all night studying so she could keep up with her classes.

After law school, Jordan ventured into politics. She did so at a time when any woman, let alone an African-American woman, had a slim chance of victory.

Jordan finally won an election on her third try. She became the first African-American woman to serve as a Texas state senator.

In 1972, Jordan became the first African-American woman from the South ever elected to the United States Congress. She served three terms before retiring in 1978 to become a college professor. "I have a tremendous amount of faith in my own capacity," she said after winning her first congressional election. "I know how to read and write and think, so I have no fear."[7]

Yet sometimes even Jordan herself was amazed at what she achieved. "Sometimes I just stare in the mirror and look at myself and I say, 'Barbara, by golly you've done okay. It wasn't easy but you've done okay.'"[8]

How did Barbara Jordan, a disadvantaged young girl who experienced racism, sexism, and segregation, become a much-admired woman? Her story begins in 1936 in a cramped brick house in Houston, Texas.

2

LAST, BUT NEVER LEAST

he brick house in Houston, Texas, overflowed with people. It was here that Benjamin and Arlyne Jordan lived with their two young daughters, Rose Mary and Bennie. Benjamin Jordan's father, Charles, and his father's wife, Alice, also shared the living space.

On February 21, 1936, a seventh person was added to the household. On that day, Arlyne Jordan gave birth to another baby girl. This daughter was christened Barbara Charline. The child's middle name was derived from her paternal grandfather. He was a church deacon.

There was nothing in Barbara's surroundings to suggest she was destined for success. During her early childhood, America was in the throes of the Great Depression. This was a time of economic crisis. Many banks and businesses had failed, and millions of Americans were out of work. Benjamin Jordan was fortunate: He worked in a warehouse and was a Baptist minister as well. Nonetheless, it was difficult to make ends meet.

"We were poor, but so was everyone around us, so we did not notice it," Barbara recalled years later. "We were never hungry, and we always had a place to stay."[1]

The Jordan home was in one of the largest African-American ghettos in Houston. Roads in the neighborhood were unpaved, and there were no streetlights.[2] The house itself was very small, with seven people sharing one bathroom. Barbara and her two sisters slept together in a foldout bed in the dining room. Later, when the family's finances improved somewhat, Benjamin Jordan constructed a third bedroom in the house to ease the crowded conditions. It was not until Barbara was in high school that Benjamin Jordan moved his family into a home of their own. The frame house on Campbell Street was painted pink, the family's favorite color.

Like other African Americans of her generation, Barbara lived in a segregated society. (Segregation is the policy, by law and custom, of separating people by race, in this case blacks and whites.) In the 1890s, the United States Supreme Court had ruled that states could impose segregation as long as blacks and whites were offered equal facilities. This ruling became the "separate but equal" doctrine.

As a result of segregation, blacks in many states were not allowed to attend the same schools, shop at the same stores, eat at the same restaurants, or use the same restrooms as white people. The facilities for blacks often were inferior to those offered to whites. For the most part, African Americans were considered second-class citizens. Barbara recalled years later:

> I did not think it was right for blacks to be in one place and whites in another and never shall the two meet. . . . There was just something about that that didn't feel right to me. And I wanted that to change, but I also had these feelings that it was going to be this way for a long, long time, and that nobody was going to be able to do anything to change it.[3]

She added that segregation "was the way of life, and if you were fortunate and would just drive hard enough, you might be able to break out of it a little bit."[4]

As an adult, Barbara was, indeed, able to break out of the cycle of prejudice and poverty. This was largely due to the influence of her family. Although Barbara and her sisters grew up in difficult circumstances, parental love and guidance were plentiful. Benjamin Jordan, who had attended Tuskegee College in

Alabama, was very strict. He did not allow his daughters to see movies or attend school dances.

"He never struck us, but the way he talked to us when he was displeased was more of a punishment than mother's spankings," Barbara's sister Rose Mary said. "Just to have him question you frightened you to the point of never doing it again."[5]

Benjamin Jordan demanded that Barbara and her sisters study hard and learn how to think for themselves. He became angry if they brought home even one B on their report cards.[6] A language lover, he emphasized proper diction and precise enunciation. Arlyne Jordan also placed importance on articulation. She was a well-known speaker at the family's church, the Good Hope Missionary Baptist Church. Barbara would be profoundly influenced by her parents' emphasis on language skills. As an adult, her deep, booming voice would be likened to the imagined voice of God.

Barbara recalled that her father often boasted to his friends about his daughters' behavior. "He would say, 'They don't smoke, they don't dance, they don't play cards, they don't go to the movies,'" she said. ". . . I thought, 'How can he go around bragging about the fact that he has three freaks?'"[7]

The Jordan family attended Good Hope every Sunday. Barbara and her sisters were enthusiastic singers in the choir. Afterward, the family often ate dinner with their maternal grandfather. Grandfather John Ed Patten owned a junk business, and Barbara enjoyed helping him organize his various treasures. She also rode old bicycles that Patten found and repaired for her.

Before Barbara was born, Patten owned a candy store. One day, he accidentally shot a white police officer while chasing a would-be robber out of his establishment. An all-white jury convicted Patten of assault with intent to murder. He was sentenced to ten years in prison. Eventually, Patten was pardoned along with other African Americans who had been wrongly convicted of crimes in Texas. However, the experience became folklore in the family and brought racism home to Barbara and her family.[8]

It was Benjamin Jordan's rules—to think, to get good grades, and to speak properly—that most influenced his youngest daughter when she entered Phillis Wheatley High School. The school, for African-American students only, was named for a former slave who became a noted poet.

Barbara thrived at Phillis Wheatley. She was an excellent student, with physical education her worst subject. At the same time, the teenager was very sociable. In fact, she did not consider herself a serious student. Barbara received her driver's license when she was only fourteen years old. When she was not tutoring friends in subjects such as chemistry and geometry, she took them for rides in her father's car. Sometimes, she got into trouble for talking in class instead of listening to teachers.

Talking, in fact, became Barbara's special talent. She joined the speech team at her high school and won many awards for her oratorical skills. It was not only the content of her speeches, but also the manner in which she delivered them, that so impressed and captivated her audiences.

In 1952, her senior year, Barbara won first place in a statewide speech contest for African-American students. Then she traveled to Chicago, Illinois, to compete in the national competition. Her topic was, "Is the Necessity for a Higher Education More in Demand Today Than a Decade Ago?" Barbara, of course, argued that it was. She earned first place. Because of these achievements as well as her top grades, Barbara was named her school's Girl of the Year for 1952.

As Barbara neared the end of her high school years, she began thinking about a career. Like her sisters before her, Barbara would attend college. Eventually, Rose Mary and Bennie both became music teachers. However, Barbara was unsure what she should study. She knew she wanted to be "something unusual" instead of following her mother's career of being a homemaker.[9]

"For awhile, I thought about becoming a pharmacist," Barbara said. "But then I thought, whoever heard of an outstanding pharmacist?"[10]

One day, Edith Sampson came to speak at Barbara's school. Sampson was an African-American lawyer. Barbara was fascinated by Sampson's talk, which she delivered in "a very deep and resonant voice," as Barbara recalled.[11] The teenager decided that she, too, would become a lawyer.

It was a bold choice. During Barbara's youth, it was very rare for women to become attorneys. They encountered sexism in the classroom as well as the workplace. For an African-American woman in a segregated society, the experience was bound to be even more difficult. In fact, of all the lawyers in 1950, fewer than one hundred were African-American females.[12] Barbara was undaunted, however.

"The impediments were there, had I chosen to focus on them and become discouraged by them," Barbara recalled. "But I was always convinced that I could wipe those out, or overcome them, or turn them into advantages.[13]

Benjamin Jordan supported his youngest child's decision. "There was never any notion that we couldn't achieve because of race or poverty," Barbara recalled. "My father always said, 'I'll support you as far as you want to go.'"[14]

So it was decided. With her father's blessing as well as financial support, Barbara would attend law school. First, however, she needed to complete four years of undergraduate work. In the fall of 1952, after graduating in the top five percent of her high school class and only sixteen years old, Barbara enrolled at Texas Southern University in Houston.

3

A SEGREGATED NATION

To cut down on expenses, and also because of her young age, Barbara lived at home while attending Texas Southern University in Houston. She studied political science and history and earned top grades. When she was not reading textbooks or attending classes, she was involved with the activities of a sorority, Delta Sigma Theta. Barbara paid the membership dues by cleaning houses and baby-sitting.

Barbara also joined the all-black college's debate team. The coach, Dr. Tom Freeman, was reluctant to let Barbara join. It was not her ability, however, that concerned him. Rather, it was her gender. The team, which traveled all over the country to compete against other colleges, had never before had a female student on it.

In response, Barbara consciously "defeminized" herself. She cut her hair, gained weight, and wore flat shoes and sensible clothes. It was this new, "no-nonsense" Barbara that participated on the team. The image she created for herself would be the one associated with her for the rest of her life.

Traveling with the debate team opened Barbara's eyes to the realities of a segregated nation. The African-American students could not eat in restaurants or sleep in motels in many cities and towns through which they traveled. They compensated by eating picnic dinners in the TSU parking lot before leaving on trips. They also packed snacks to eat in Freeman's car. Sometimes, they drove through the night so they would not have to worry about finding accommodations.

Many southern white teams would not debate blacks, so Barbara and the team traveled to integrated cities in the North and Northeast. While in New England, Barbara visited Boston University. She decided that when the time came, she would apply to Boston University's noted law school.

While a student at Texas Southern University, Barbara Jordan (front row, right) was president of the Sigma Pi Alpha Forensic and Dialectical Symposium. The purpose of the club was to help students gain excellence in speech, debate, and oratory.

In 1954, Barbara had her first experience with integration in the South. The TSU team participated in a debate at the all-white Baylor University in Texas. Barbara won first place in the oratory category. This win advanced her to a competition at the University of Chicago.

On that trip Barbara recalled:

> I felt as if I had left the old country and moved into some new dynamic scene. We could go in the front door of hotels and go in the front door of these restaurants and sit down and have a meal. It gave us an appreciation for what integration would mean for us if it ever came South.[1]

Also in 1954, a historic ruling paved the way for integration across the United States. In *Brown* v. *Board of Education of Topeka*, the Supreme Court determined that segregation in public schools deprived African Americans of equal education. The following year, the Supreme Court ordered schools across the country to integrate "with all deliberate speed."

An incident in 1955 marked the beginning of mass black protest in the civil rights movement. That December, a seamstress in Montgomery, Alabama, refused to give her seat on a city bus to a white person. The woman, Rosa Parks, broke a law granting preferential seating to whites. African Americans in the city were outraged over the treatment of Parks. Led by Reverend Martin Luther King, Jr., they organized boycotts of city buses. Eventually, the law was overturned. Many more struggles occurred in cities all over the South before the Civil Rights Act of 1964 eliminated legal segregation.

Barbara watched the events of the mid-1950s unfold with interest. She believed integration could be achieved with less racial discord if blacks proved they could make it in a "white man's world." Barbara intended to become one of the African Americans to help integration along. She started by gaining admission to Boston University.

In 1956, Barbara graduated with honors from Texas Southern University. Then she moved away from home for the first time in her life. Classes at Boston University started in the fall. Barbara was one of only five women out of almost six hundred students in the freshman law class. She was the only African-American student.

"I had ambition, and I've always been willing to work, however many hours a day would be required for me to work," Barbara recalled.[2] Her willingness to spend countless hours at a task would prove invaluable as Barbara encountered the challenges of law school.

4

UP ALL NIGHT

In high school and college, Barbara Jordan found it fairly easy to get good grades. She did not have to spend a lot of time studying notes and reading textbooks. It was a different story when the Houston transplant joined the freshman law class at Boston University.

During those hectic, pressure-filled years, Jordan rarely slept more than three or four hours a night. As soon as classes were over, she headed for the library with a huge stack of law books in her arms. There, until the wee hours of the morning, Jordan read the cases assigned by her professors. She often had to read them again and again before she completely understood them. Eventually, Jordan joined a study group made up of other African-American students from upper-level classes. She found it easier to understand the material if she was able to discuss it with others.

At the end of her first year in law school, Jordan flew home. It was her first airplane trip. The exhausted student prepared her father for the worst, telling him that she was unsure whether she had passed all of her classes. But when her grades came in the mail, Jordan was relieved. She had made it through the first year. The next two years of school would be easier, but not much.

Jordan came to believe that her earlier education had been inferior to the education received by her white classmates. The Supreme Court was right in *Brown* v. *Board of Education*, Jordan thought. Separate was not equal.

"No matter what kind of face you put on it or how many frills you attached to it, separate was not equal," she said. "I was doing sixteen years of remedial work in thinking."[1]

Jordan had other pressures besides academics. For one, she had very little money. Her parents paid for her tuition, room, and board, and her sister Rose Mary bought her books. In addition, Rose Mary and Bennie, both of whom were now teachers, each gave Barbara $10 a month for spending money.

Nonetheless, there were many times that Jordan could not participate in social events because she could not afford it. Nor could she travel home to Houston for the holidays. In later years, Jordan developed a reputation for being unreasonably frugal, even stingy. Perhaps that dates back to her years in law school when she simply did not have any money to spend.

Despite being the only African-American student in her class, Jordan did not encounter much racism. Sexism, however, was rampant. she recalled:

> The professors did not call on the "ladies" very much [in class]. There were certain favored people who always got called on, and then on some rare occasions a professor would come in and would announce, "We're going to have Ladies Day today." We were just tolerated.[2]

Some of Jordan's female classmates could not handle the pressures and left school. When Jordan received her degree from Boston University in 1959, she was one of only two women left in her graduating class. Law school was a struggle, but Jordan believed the experience taught her how to think. She had learned to read, to reason, and to defend her opinions.

Jordan thought seriously of settling down in Boston. She felt more comfortable in the integrated city. She even passed the Massachusetts bar exam. The new lawyer intended to open a practice there. In the end, however, Jordan decided to return home to Houston. She missed her family and believed that her connections and lifelong friendships there could help her career.

Jordan passed the Texas bar exam and moved back into her parents' home in Houston. She barely had enough money to buy business cards that read "Barbara Jordan, Attorney at Law."[3] The new lawyer also lacked the funds to rent office space.

So Jordan set up her law practice in her parents' dining room. She supplemented her income by working as an administrative assistant to a county judge. It would take Jordan almost three years to save enough money to move her business out of her parents' home.

In 1960, Jordan became involved in politics. A young, handsome United States senator from Massachusetts named John F. Kennedy was running for president of the United States. Kennedy, a Democrat, strongly supported the civil rights movement. His Republican opponent was Vice President Richard Nixon.

Jordan, a Kennedy supporter, volunteered her services locally. At first, she performed simple chores such as stuffing envelopes at the headquarters of the

In 1960, Barbara Jordan became involved in politics by working on the Kennedy presidential campaign.

Harris County, Texas, Democratic Committee. Soon, however, her oratory skills led her to other endeavors.

One night, a Democratic speaker called in sick. He was scheduled to talk to the congregation of a local African-American church. Jordan was asked to substitute for him. Her imposing figure, deep voice, crisp enunciation, and simple yet meaningful message moved her audience. Jordan recalled:

> I was startled with the impact I had on people. Those people were just as turned on and excited as if some of the head candidates had been there to talk about the issues. When I got back to the local headquarters that night . . . they said, "Look, we're going to have to take you off the . . . lists and the envelopes and put you on the speaking circuit."[4]

Jordan began lecturing all over Houston. She urged African Americans to register to vote and to support the Democratic ticket. The enthusiastic responses she received energized and encouraged her.

In November 1960, Kennedy narrowly beat Nixon to become the thirty-fifth president of the United States. Jordan began thinking that perhaps she, too, would "make a move in this direction."[5] Jordan decided that instead of working behind the scenes, she would actually run for public office. That task would prove to be one of her greatest challenges.

5

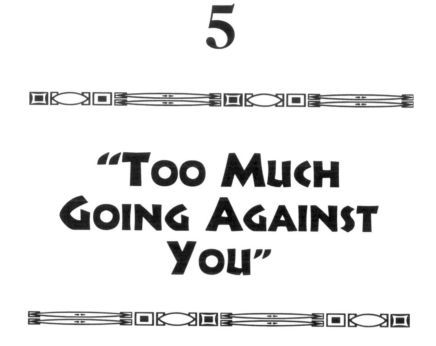

"Too Much Going Against You"

 arbara Jordan never was the type of person to give up easily. That quality proved to be invaluable when she decided to run for public office. In the 1960 presidential election, Jordan stumped throughout Houston for the Democratic ticket of John F. Kennedy and fellow Texan Lyndon B. Johnson. Now, Democratic party officials in Harris County were urging Jordan to declare herself a candidate for the Texas House of Representatives.

"There are people out there who really think you can make some kind of difference to them," Jordan recalled. "So you start to think you *can* make a difference. That motivated me."[1] Jordan decided to enter the 1962 race.

The novice politician was a candidate in Harris County, which included her hometown of Houston. The county's million-plus eligible voters were a diverse group economically, socially, and racially. Jordan needed to reach as many of these voters as she could. For a candidate without strong financial backing, this was extremely difficult. In fact, Jordan did not even have enough money to pay the $500 filing fee for the election. She had to borrow the money.

Jordan's opponent, a white lawyer named Willis Whatley, was well financed. He spent thousands of dollars advertising on billboards and television. Jordan could not afford those campaign expenses. Years later, she said the amount of money needed to run an election "border[s] on obscenity. When I ran my first race . . . we . . . had to raise $12,000, $15,000, $20,000. That was hard to come by for me, a person without independent resources."[2]

Despite her lack of funds, Jordan was optimistic about her chances. "I believed that I was more articulate than my opponent, and sensitive to people's needs and aspirations," she recalled. "These qualities, I felt, would help me overcome the odds."[3]

She added, "I felt that if politicians were believable, and pressed the flesh to the maximum extent possible, the people would overlook race, sex, and poverty—and elect me. They did not."[4]

Though Jordan was well qualified and worked hard to win, she lost to Whatley by about twenty thousand votes. It was a frustrating experience, particularly after a political expert gave her some disturbing advice. "You've got too much going against you," he told Jordan. "You're black, you're a woman, and you're large. People don't really like that image."[5]

Jordan refused to believe voters were turned off by her looks. She resolved to run for the state legislature again in 1964. In the meantime, she continued working as an administrative assistant to a county judge. Her private practice was doing so well that she moved her office out of her parents' home and into a building downtown.

When it was time to begin campaigning for the 1964 election, Jordan realized she needed more than good intentions. "It was clear . . . that if I was to win . . . I had to persuade the moneyed and politically influential interests either to support me or remain neutral," Jordan said.[6]

As she did in her first election, Jordan met and spoke with as many voters as she possibly could. This time, however, she also contacted the publishers of Houston's two major newspapers. She made an appeal: If they did not want to endorse her candidacy, then at least remain neutral and not support her opponent, either.

One publisher heeded Jordan's request and made no endorsement. The other newspaper publisher, however, endorsed her opponent. Jordan lost the election, though she received more votes than she had in her previous run.

With her second loss in two tries, Jordan did some soul-searching. Was politics her destiny? She even considered moving someplace where it was not considered unusual for an African-American woman to run for public office. Finally, she decided to stay in Texas. She continued to work in her law practice. However, in 1965 she resigned her position with the county judge. Then she became director of a foundation to help the unemployed.

Despite her two losses, Jordan was determined to pursue a political career. Her parents were supportive of their youngest daughter, but they often told her that she should get married. Both Rose Mary and Bennie had husbands. However, the youngest Jordan daughter did not think she could handle both a political career and a family life. She believed that she had to choose. She decided politics was the most important thing to her.

Meanwhile, events unfolding in American society would prove to have a profound effect on Jordan, not only as an African American but also as a candidate for public office. In 1963, hundreds of thousands of people held a civil rights rally in Washington, D.C., known as the March on Washington. It was here that Martin Luther King, Jr., delivered his celebrated "I Have a Dream" speech. King declared in a booming voice:

> I have a dream that one day this nation will rise up and live out the true meaning of its creed: "We hold these truths to be self-evident: that all men are created equal." I have a dream . . . that my four little children will one day live in a nation where they will not be judged by the color of their skin but by the content of their character.[7]

The next year, the United States Congress passed the Civil Rights Act of 1964. This federal law banned segregation in public facilities and guaranteed equal employment. Also that year, the Twenty-fourth Amendment to the Constitution was adopted. This law prohibited poll taxes for federal elections. When African Americans won the right to vote in 1870, many southern states began requiring poll taxes in order to prevent African Americans from exercising that right. More than six hundred thousand people registered to vote in Texas after that state abolished its poll tax.[8]

Further strides were made with the Voting Rights Act of 1965. This eliminated literacy tests and other devices that traditionally had been used to prevent

African Americans from voting. That same year, Harris County was divided into voting districts. As a result of a 1962 Supreme Court decision, *Baker* v. *Carr*, state legislatures were apportioned to provide equal protection for all citizens. Now, Americans in each district would vote for their own representatives, instead of voting for candidates countywide.

With reapportionment, Houston was awarded ten new legislative seats. One of those seats was in the newly created Eleventh District, where Jordan lived. The district had many African Americans, Hispanics, and white union workers. These were the voters who had supported Jordan in her two previous campaigns. The time was right, Jordan believed, for a third try at public office. She would run for one of the new seats in the Texas Senate.

Another Democrat, Charles Whitfield, also was interested in the new Senate seat. Whitfield was a white liberal who had served in the Texas Congress for eight years.

Jordan and Whitfield squared off for the Democratic primary. Jordan campaigned exhaustively. She mailed sample ballots and explicit voting instructions to each African-American home in her district. She also spoke to white civic groups, extolling the need for minimum-wage provisions and lower auto-insurance rates.[9] Whitfield also ran hard. His slogan—"Can a white man win?"—was considered by many to be racist.[10]

One day, the white-ruled Harris County Democrats Committee called a meeting to decide which candidate to support. Jordan said to the committee, "I ran a race in 1962. You endorsed me and I lost. I ran a race in 1964. You endorsed me and I lost. I want you to know I have no intention of being a three-time loser."[11]

One of Jordan's supporters also spoke. "If we elect Charley [Whitfield], we're electing another senator," labor lawyer Chris Dixon said. "If we elect Barbara Jordan, we're beginning the modern history of Texas."[12] Jordan received the group's endorsement.

The primary was held on May 8, 1966. This time, finally, it was Jordan's turn to triumph. She beat Whitfield by a margin of two to one. Since there was no Republican opponent to face the following November, Jordan's victory to the Texas Senate was assured.

It was a historic election. Jordan became the first African American elected to the Texas Senate since the 1880s and the first African-American woman elected. Also, her victory crossed racial lines. Along with carrying the black vote, she earned a substantial number of white votes. "The election results showed . . . that capable Negro office seekers can win the white support necessary for victory," *Time* magazine reported shortly after the primary.[13]

Jordan was sworn into office in January 1967 in the state capital of Austin. Her family, friends, relatives, and countless other supporters came to witness the historic event.

Jordan recalled:

> Although demonstrations are not permitted, my supporters cheered when I walked onto the floor. I looked up at them and covered my lips with my index finger. They became quiet instantly, but continued to communicate their support by simply smiling. Finally, I had won the right to represent a portion of the people of Texas.[14]

The moment was sweet. However, Jordan realized that a lot of work was ahead of her. There were thirty-one state senators, and thirty of them were white men. To be an effective legislator, then, Jordan would need to learn the written as well as unwritten rules.

6

THE STATE SENATE

s Texas's first African-American state senator in about eighty years, Jordan knew she would be under great scrutiny by friends and foes alike. The new legislator vowed to fulfill the expectations of her supporters and to silence her critics. Jordan recalled:

> There was some feeling that I would come in with bombast, mount the stump, and curse the system. So I came in quietly. I attended the committee meetings, studied the legislation, [and] developed professional friendships among senior members who felt most threatened by my presence. I gained their confidence.[1]

> I singled out the most influential and powerful members and was determined to gain their respect.[2]

As she did in law school, Jordan studied diligently. She became familiar with the issues as well as with the opinions and emotions surrounding them. Jordan also learned that if she wanted to be effective, she needed to use the rules to her advantage.

For example, a senator once sponsored a bill that Jordan believed would make voter registration difficult for African Americans and other minorities. The senator needed twenty-one votes for the bill to be considered. Jordan needed ten of her colleagues to join her in opposing it. Jordan recalled:

> I made a list of ten senators who were in my political debt. I went to each one and said I was calling in my chit. I needed their votes in order to keep the . . . proposal from Senate deliberation.
>
> Armed with ten commitments, I went to [the senator who sponsored the bill] and asked when he planned to bring the bill to the floor of the Senate. He smiled, but with resignation, and said, "I, too, can count; the bill is dead, Barbara."[3]

A few months after her election, President Lyndon B. Johnson invited Jordan to Washington, D.C., to discuss a fair-housing bill. Like Jordan, Johnson was a Democrat and a Texan. He had ascended from the vice presidency to the presidency in November 1963 after John F. Kennedy was assassinated. After

Barbara Jordan won election to the Texas State Senate in 1966.

completing President Kennedy's term, Johnson had gone on to win the presidential election of 1964.

Jordan had great respect for Johnson's commitment to equal rights, and they developed a close political friendship. The president invited the state senator to several events at the White House. He also appointed her to an economic commission. In a few years, Jordan's relationship with Johnson would help pave her way to higher office.

During her six years in the state senate, Jordan compiled an impressive record. She helped defeat a sales tax that she believed would unfairly burden poor people. Her amendment to the Omnibus Crime Control and Safe Streets Act funded programs for citizens to help fight crime.

Jordan sponsored a bill establishing the Texas Fair Employment Practices Commission. She supported legislation to improve the workers' compensation act. The busy senator also developed the state's first minimum wage law. It was designed to include farm workers, domestic workers, and others not covered by federal minimum-wage guarantees.

Jordan also was chairperson of the state senate's Labor and Management Committee and vice chairperson of the Legislative, Congressional, and Judicial committees. In addition, she served as a member of Youth Affairs and other committees.

Many of her white male colleagues had not expected much of Jordan. Because of her looks, some of them referred to her as a "mammy." This was an offensive slang word in the South for a black woman who takes care of white children. In fact, one of the state senators always referred to Jordan as "the nigger mammy washerwoman."[4]

However, Jordan's colleagues came to realize that the African-American woman was an intelligent, articulate lawmaker who took her job very seriously. At the end of Jordan's first term, they sponsored a resolution commending her contributions. She was named Outstanding Freshman Senator. The resolution was sponsored by Senator Dorsey Hardeman of San Angelo. He had been one of the senators who had not expected much from Jordan. In fact, when she first came to the senate, the conservative lawmaker did not want to have anything to do with her.[5]

In 1968, Jordan ran unopposed for a second term in the state senate. "If one wanted to think up the three handicaps with which one could enter a know-nothing, reactionary state senate of those days, it would be a person of liberal persuasion, a woman, and a black," recalled Robert Cochran, former chief editorial writer for the *Houston Chronicle*. "Yet [Jordan's] intelligence and her commanding

On June 10, 1972, Barbara Jordan became governor of Texas for the day. She is shown here with Judge Andrew Jefferson of Harris County (left) and an unidentified Texas official.

personality got her to the point where she had the Senate eating out of her hand."[6]

During Jordan's senate career, more than half of all the bills she submitted were made into law. She became known as the most powerful African American in Texas politics.[7] Her hometown was so proud of her that October 1, 1971, was proclaimed Barbara Jordan Day in Houston.

In March 1972, Jordan was elected president pro tempore of the Texas legislature. With this honor, she became the first African-American woman to preside over a legislative body in the United States. One of her duties was to act as governor when both the governor and lieutenant governor were out of the state. This was arranged so that on June 10, 1972, Jordan became governor for the day.

It was a festive, fun-filled occasion for the proud state senator and her family. However, it also was marked by tragedy. The day started with a breakfast at the governor's mansion in Austin. All of Jordan's family was in attendance except for her father, Benjamin. He had a heart condition and was resting so that he could enjoy the other festivities planned later in the day.

After breakfast and a welcoming ceremony, a reception for Jordan was held at the capital. The room was packed with friends and colleagues who brought gifts and good wishes to the "new governor." During

As Texas governor for the day, Barbara Jordan was given a reception at the capital, attended by friends and colleagues.

this event, Jordan learned that her father's condition had worsened. He had been taken to the hospital. However, Barbara Jordan was led to believe there was no cause for worry.

Choral and band groups from Jordan's high school and college entertained during a barbecue lunch. After that, Benjamin Jordan's youngest daughter went to visit the man who had been instrumental in pushing her to succeed.

Benjamin Jordan had suffered a stroke. He was unable to speak. However, he grinned when his daughter told him that she was glad he saw her as governor. The next day, Benjamin Jordan died. "If my father had the option of choosing a time to die, he would have chosen that day," Barbara Jordan later told a friend.[8]

Benjamin Jordan saw his daughter become governor, if only for a day. Had he lived a few months longer, he would have witnessed her most important victory of all. In 1972, Barbara Jordan set her sights on Washington, D.C. She campaigned for a seat in the United States House of Representatives.

7

RUNNING FOR CONGRESS

he United States Congress is made up of two chambers: the Senate and the House of Representatives. In the Senate, two people are elected from each state to guarantee equal representation. In the House, seats are apportioned based on each state's population. States with high populations have more representatives than the less populous states.

After a census in 1970, voting districts in Texas were redrawn. This resulted in the creation of the Eighteenth Congressional District. It was about 50

percent white, 35 percent Hispanic, and 15 percent black. Some of the new district's population was carved out of Barbara Jordan's old state senatorial district. Jordan's home now fell in the boundaries of the Eighteenth District.

An election was set for the fall of 1972 to choose a United States congressional representative for the new district. Jordan decided it was time to leave state politics behind and enter the national scene.

Jordan faced three other African-American opponents in the Democratic primary for the new congressional seat. One of them, state representative Curtis Graves, ran a particularly nasty campaign. He accused Jordan of helping create the new district so she would be able to run for national office. Graves believed the boundaries of the new district undermined minority power in the old state senatorial district.

Graves said Jordan was "the best black congressman money can buy."[1] He also called her an "Uncle Tom." This derogatory term referred to African Americans who either passively accepted a position of inferiority or who cooperated with white leaders instead of working with other African Americans for change.

Jordan defended her way of working within the system instead of fighting it. "All blacks are militants in their guts," she said. "But militancy is expressed in different ways."[2] She also said, "I went to Austin to work, not to crusade."[3] This meant that she believed it was more important to concentrate on specific pieces of legislation instead of taking general positions on issues.

Despite the controversies, Jordan received widespread support for her candidacy, including an endorsement from the *Houston Chronicle*. The conservative newspaper called the Democrat "an eloquent spokesman—perhaps the most effective in our state's history—against human injustice."[4]

A famous Texas politician even got involved in the race. As president, Lyndon B. Johnson had been a champion of minorities and disadvantaged Americans. He established government programs that provided job training, improved housing conditions, and expanded educational opportunities.

Yet Johnson also had increased American involvement in the Vietnam War. His predecessors, presidents Dwight D. Eisenhower and John F. Kennedy, had sent money and military advisers to South Vietnam to help them fight communist North Vietnam. When Johnson became president, he began sending American soldiers to actually help the South Vietnamese fight. By the end of 1967, almost five hundred thousand American troops were in South Vietnam. Money that had been marked for American domestic programs was now being spent on the war effort.

Johnson faced opposition from his fellow Democratic lawmakers as well as growing public disapproval. The frustrated president decided not to run for reelection in 1968. His vice president, Hubert Humphrey, became the Democratic candidate. Due in part to his association with Johnson's war policies, he was defeated by the Republican candidate, Richard M. Nixon.

After leaving office, Johnson returned to his ranch in Texas. However, he was pleased to return to the spotlight to help his friend Barbara Jordan win a congressional seat. Johnson attended fund-raising dinners held in Jordan's honor. He publicly said the African-American woman was "the epitome of the new politics" in the nation and that she "proved black is beautiful before we knew what it meant."[5]

On primary day in May 1972, Jordan won more than four times as many votes as Graves and her two other African-American opponents combined. She was jubilant but tried not to get her hopes up. "It's a Presidential year, and more Republicans may show up" at the polls in November, Jordan said during her victory celebration. "I can't take any chances—not after this."[6]

There was no need for Jordan to worry, however. The following November, she handily beat Republican

Lyndon Johnson attended fund-raising dinners in Barbara Jordan's honor during her 1972 congressional campaign.

Paul Merritt. This victory marked another "first" for the remarkable Jordan. She became the first African-American woman from the South elected to the United States Congress. Jordan, who had endured poverty and prejudice with her head held high, was on her way to Washington, D.C.

8

THE NATIONAL SPOTLIGHT

he same year that Jordan won a congressional seat, Richard M. Nixon was reelected president of the United States. The Republican was a veteran politician. He had been a United States congressperson in the 1940s. Then he was Dwight D. Eisenhower's vice president for two terms in the 1950s. As president, Nixon made historic trips to the People's Republic of China and the Soviet Union. He also brought the Vietnam War to an end.

Despite his accomplishments, Nixon's legacy became the Watergate scandal. He resigned in disgrace in August 1974, leaving a nation disillusioned with politics as well as politicians. Yet Nixon's darkest days became Barbara Jordan's time to shine. A speech she made shortly before the president's resignation proved to the American public that not everyone in Washington, D.C., took public service lightly. Jordan's words turned her into a political folk hero.

The Watergate scandal actually began in June 1972. Five men working to reelect Nixon were arrested for breaking into the headquarters of the Democratic National Committee. The headquarters was located at the Watergate Hotel in Washington, D.C.

The *Washington Post* newspaper ran a small article about the break-in, but it did not attract much attention. During the next two years, reporters Carl Bernstein and Bob Woodward would uncover startling details that finally caused the public to take notice.

In the meantime, Jordan arrived in Washington, D.C., in January 1973 and was appointed as a member of the House Judiciary Committee. Prior to that, she and some other new legislators had gathered for a retreat at Harvard University in Massachusetts. There, they learned more about how Congress works. Both the House of Representatives and the Senate organize their members into committees. These committees study various issues, recommend the course of action to take, and work to pass laws. Committee assignments are made by legislative leaders.

Jordan was interested in working on one of two major committees: Armed Forces, which deals with military issues, and Judiciary. "All civil rights legislation, questions regarding the administration of justice, [and] constitutional amendments are handled by the Judiciary committee," Jordan said.[1]

She asked her political mentor, Lyndon B. Johnson, for advice. He recommended Jordan try to obtain a spot on the Judiciary Committee. Then the former president made some telephone calls. With Johnson's glowing recommendation of his fellow Texan and Democrat, Jordan landed the coveted spot. It was considered a very prestigious assignment for a new congressperson.

Helping Jordan would be one of Johnson's final acts. He died of a heart attack at his Texas ranch in 1973. Jordan gave a speech on the House floor in his honor, noting how much the former president had done to advance equality for African Americans. Jordan called Johnson her political mentor as well as her friend.

As she had done during her days in law school as well as the Texas Senate, Congressperson Jordan spent long hours studying the issues. She also quickly developed strong working relationships with her fellow legislators. Jordan's political skills were impressive. "There was no learning process for Barbara Jordan," said one person familiar with the ways of Washington. "She seemed to know the day she got here how experienced Congressmen act, how they get heard. She's unbelievably savvy politically."[2]

Those skills would be put to good use as Nixon's troubles grew. The nation learned from televised hearings in the United States Senate that the president had tape-recorded conversations in his White House office during the period of the Watergate break-in. Nixon refused to release the tapes. When he finally did so under court order, the tapes proved the president had known that men working for him had tried to block an investigation. Nixon also had ordered staff members to cover up the break-in.

The House Judiciary Committee already had dealt with the confirmation of a new vice president, Gerald Ford. The former vice president, Spiro T. Agnew, resigned in October 1973 following charges of income tax evasion. Now, the committee turned its attention to the president's role in Watergate. The same month that Agnew resigned, Jordan and the other members of the House Judiciary Committee began considering possible impeachment procedures against the president.

An impeachment is a formal charge of wrongdoing against a public official. The House of Representatives votes on impeachment, but the Senate actually tries the case. Only one other president in United States history has been impeached. In the 1860s, Andrew

Johnson was charged with illegally firing a government official. He was acquitted by one vote in the Senate.

In May 1974, the Judiciary Committee began formal hearings on the possible impeachment of President Nixon. Jordan and her fellow committee members spent the next ten weeks gathering evidence. Key to the case were transcripts of the tape-recorded conversations.

Jordan devoted herself to her work. Every night, after putting in a full day at the office, she took home notebooks that outlined evidence against the president. She studied them intently. "I *lived* the impeachment matter," Jordan said. "It was a 24-hour-a-day engagement where I was concerned."[3]

In the beginning, Jordan found the idea of impeachment difficult to comprehend. She also was uncomfortable with her task. She said:

> I have the same high regard for the office of the president as the majority of Americans. He is a figure who towers above all other figures in the world. Certainly no one could seriously consider forcing the president to leave office before his term expired. This feeling stayed with me a long time.[4]

As Jordan delved deeper and deeper into the notebooks, she realized that Nixon had, indeed, committed offenses. Most of the almost forty other members of the Judiciary Committee, Republicans and Democrats alike, came to the same conclusion.

In May 1974, the House Judiciary Committee began formal hearings on the possible impeachment of President Nixon. Here, Barbara Jordan is shown with fellow committee members.

In July 1974, the committee began debating articles of impeachment against Nixon. The debate was televised, and each member spoke for fifteen minutes. One after another, they talked about how they felt about the issue.

Most of the members began their statements by quoting the Preamble of the Constitution:

> We, the people of the United States, in order to form a more perfect union, establish justice, insure domestic tranquillity, provide for the common defense, promote the general welfare, and secure the blessings of liberty to ourselves and our posterity, do ordain and establish this Constitution for the United States of America.

Jordan's turn to speak came on July 25, 1974, the second night of the televised debate. She wore a bright orange dress and delivered her speech with crisp diction that would have made her father proud. Viewers all across the nation were mesmerized. *The New York Times* later would describe it as "the moment Barbara Jordan burst on the national scene."[5]

Jordan began her speech by saying that "we the people" was an eloquent beginning for the Constitution. However, she added that when the document was written in 1787, Jordan, as an African-American woman, "was not included in that 'We, the People,' I felt somehow for many years that George Washington and Alexander Hamilton just left me out by mistake," she said. "But through the process of amendment,

Barbara Jordan's turn to speak regarding the possible Nixon impeachment came on July 25, 1974.

interpretation, and court decisions, I have finally been included in 'We the people.'"

"My faith in the Constitution is whole, it is complete, it is total," she continued. "I am not going to sit here and be an idle spectator to the diminution, the subversion, the destruction of the Constitution."[6]

In her speech, Jordan outlined the committee's findings. She added that the evidence was so strong against Nixon that if the committee did not vote to impeach, "then perhaps the eighteenth-century Constitution should be abandoned to a twentieth-century paper shredder."[7]

"It was stunning," *The New York Times* later reported. "The words had rolled from her lips in that formal speaking voice of hers, like a Shakespearean actor, some said, or, as one of those in the audience remarked at the time, 'as if the gates of heaven had opened.'"[8]

Later, Jordan would explain the reasoning behind her decision to impeach. She said:

> Listen, I get goose pimples over the National Anthem and "God Bless America." I don't apologize for it. I feel very keenly about the necessity for this country to survive . . . having as its supreme law a constitution which remains inviolate. I feel this quite strongly.
>
> The long-range hope I have for this country is that it will grow stronger and that everybody can feel that they're in it, that it really does belong to us. There are many of my constituents who are black and are poor who still do not feel that this country belongs to them,

that the deal they have gotten is sour. . . . I want to see the day when we—everybody—can feel like we belong here, that this country has to survive because we have to survive. . . . I'd like to see that happen, but it takes strong, moral leadership from the top.[9]

Two days after Jordan's speech, the Judiciary Committee voted to recommend that Nixon be impeached because he obstructed the investigation of Watergate and tried to cover up other unlawful activities.[10] Jordan herself voted for the impeachment, then left the room and cried.

A few days later, the committee voted for a second article of impeachment, alleging the president repeatedly misused his power and violated the constitutional rights of American citizens. They also voted to impeach on a third article that charged the president defied the committee's legal orders to turn over transcripts.

Before the full House could vote on impeachment, however, Nixon resigned. "Throughout the long and difficult period of Watergate, I have felt it was my duty to . . . make every possible effort to complete the term of office to which you elected me," Nixon said in an address to the American people on August 8, 1974.[11]

"In the past few days, however, it has become evident to me that I no longer have a strong enough political base in the Congress to justify continuing that effort," he said. " . . . I regret deeply any injuries that may have been done in the course of events that led to this decision."[12]

Nixon became the first president in the history of the United States to resign. As for Barbara Jordan, she became a hero to the American public. The day after her speech, someone in Houston erected billboards that stated, "Thank you, Barbara Jordan, for explaining the Constitution to us." She received thousands of letters praising her words. When Jordan ran for reelection in November 1974, she won with almost 85 percent of the vote.

Jordan also became a star in the Democratic party. National publications praised her intellect and strength of character. They clamored for interviews. There also was talk that the African-American woman one day would be tapped for a Cabinet post or possibly a position on the Supreme Court.

Jordan was only thirty-eight years old. Her future in politics seemed limitless.

9

BARBARA JORDAN FOR VICE PRESIDENT

he 1970s was a decade of power and influence for Barbara Jordan. In the fall election following her spectacular performance in the impeachment debate, the United States representative easily won a second term in office. Her reward was to be appointed to the Democratic Steering and Policy Committee. This "super committee" was tasked with making committee assignments for the almost three hundred Democrats in the House of Representatives. It also chose the committee chairpeople.

Jordan's assignment was considered a great honor. *The Wall Street Journal* noted that she had achieved more power after one term in office than most congresspeople could hope to obtain in their entire careers.[1] Yet those who knew Jordan realized that she had earned the assignment. "Not only does she have a good mind, but she doesn't waste words," former Representative Edward Mezvinsky, a Democrat from Iowa, said. "She knows when to come down hard and when to be gentle."[2]

Observers also were impressed with Jordan's ability to deal with the "white establishment," those congresspeople who had been in office for years, even decades. In an atmosphere where who you knew was as important as what you knew, Jordan won on both counts.

"In my view, Barbara Jordan is the most influential member of Congress," said Representative Charles Wilson, another congressperson from Texas. He added:

> If you're talking about the one person who is able to get just anybody . . . [to] stop and listen to what she has to say and convince them that she's right, then you're talking about Barbara.
>
> Now, it's obvious that Barbara is very smart, but don't forget that there are a lot of people here in Washington who are very smart. So what makes Barbara so special? It's that along with her superior intelligence and legislative skill, she also has a certain moral authority and a . . . presence, and it all comes together in a way that sort of grabs you. What Barbara

has is not something you learn and develop, it's something that God gave her, and it's something you really can't describe.[3]

As her reputation grew in Washington, D.C., Jordan attracted more attention from the public as well. In the 1970s, women were just beginning to leave their homes in significant numbers and enter the workplace. In addition, most working women had jobs in traditionally female fields such as administrative, teaching, and nursing.

So who was Barbara Jordan, this black woman who had broken into the mostly white and male world of politics? Though she tried to avoid publicity, several newspapers and magazines wrote profiles of her. They noted that her staff members called her "B.J." She worked long hours in her congressional office and almost always took home stacks of paperwork. She lived in a modest apartment in southwest Washington, D.C.

Jordan was described as a woman of great intelligence, strong character, and finely tuned political skills. Her closest friends said she was cheerful and enjoyed singing and playing the guitar at small get-togethers. Representative Patricia Schroeder of Colorado even recalled Jordan dancing the "bump" with a Marine Corps guard at a White House Christmas party in 1974.[4]

However, Jordan also was described as aloof, arrogant, and impatient. "I'm not long on patience," Jordan herself admitted. "Sometimes I'm more abrupt with people than I ought to be. I always regret it afterward."[5]

Others believed she was overly ambitious and was not above wheeling and dealing to get her way. For example, one time she gave a speech to introduce Senator Robert Byrd at a Democratic midterm convention. Byrd, from West Virginia, had voted against almost every major civil-rights bill.[6] However, a good relationship with Byrd could help Jordan out politically. "I really do believe that people change and that you can help people change more quickly, at times, by defining them," Jordan said in defense of her actions.[7]

There were other negative things said about Jordan. Some people believed she was not doing enough to help others of her race and gender. "There are times when we [African Americans] wish Barbara would stand up and be counted for something controversial or nitty-gritty," said the Reverend Bill Lawson, an African-American pastor in Houston.[8]

"I'm neither a black politician nor a woman politician," Jordan responded to critics, "just a politician, a professional politician."[9] She added that she believed she could accomplish more if she worked within the system to bring about change. "Do not call for black power or green power," she said. "Call for brain power."[10]

In 1976, Jordan was chosen to be one of two keynote speakers at the Democratic National Convention. It was a presidential election year, and the Democrats were hopeful. Republican Gerald Ford had become president after Nixon's resignation two years previously. Now he was seeking election to the nation's highest office. However, Ford had angered many voters with his pardon of former president Nixon. The time was right, many Democrats believed, to take back the presidency.

Months before the convention, Jordan was being mentioned as a possible presidential candidate. However, she told *U.S. News and World Report* that being nominated for president was "not a choice which I anticipate will be offered to me."[11] She said she might accept a nomination for vice president, "if the opportunity is there."[12] Jordan added that a white woman probably could get elected before a black woman.

Eventually, Jimmy Carter would emerge as the Democrats' top choice for president. He was a former Georgia governor who was campaigning as a political outsider. The final decision would be made at the national convention. It was held in July at Madison Square Garden in New York City.

Barbara Jordan was one of two keynote speakers at the 1976 Democratic National Convention in New York City.

The first keynote speaker was Senator John Glenn of Ohio. Glenn, a famous former astronaut, was considered the leading contender for vice president. Yet his speech failed to maintain the audience's attention. The noise in the convention hall almost drowned out Glenn's words as the three thousand delegates talked among themselves.

Then it was Jordan's turn. The crowd stood and cheered as she walked confidently onto the podium. The ovation lasted for more than three minutes. Dressed in a light-green suit, Jordan began her remarks. She noted that again she was making history. It was the first time that either an African American or a woman had been the keynote speaker at a political convention. She said:

> My presence here is one additional bit of evidence that the American Dream need not forever be deferred. Now that I have this grand distinction, what in the world am I supposed to say? I could easily spend this time praising the accomplishments of this party and attacking the Republicans, but I don't choose to do that. I could list the many problems which cause people to feel cynical, angry, frustrated. . . . I could recite these problems and then I could sit down and offer no solutions. But I don't choose to do that, either. The citizens of America expect more.[13]

Jordan went on to declare that:

> . . . those of us who are public servants must set examples. If we promise, we must deliver. If we propose, we must produce. If we ask for sacrifice, we

At the Democratic National Convention in 1976, Barbara Jordan's speech was interrupted more than twenty times by applause from the audience.

must be the first to give. If we make mistakes, we must be willing to admit them.[14]

Jordan's speech was interrupted by applause more than twenty times. It was not only her message but also her booming delivery that made it so memorable. "If God is a woman, she must sound like that," one of the admiring listeners said.[15] The next day, newspapers all over the country gave her speech excellent reviews. *Ebony* magazine, for example, called Jordan's address eloquent and insightful.[16] Talk was revived of the congressperson joining Carter on the presidential ticket.

Yet it was not to be. Jordan called a press conference to note that about fourteen other people had been mentioned as vice presidential candidates. She said it was unlikely that she, an African-American woman, would be chosen. Indeed, former United States senator from Minnesota Walter Mondale became Carter's vice presidential choice. The two men defeated Gerald Ford and his running mate, Nelson Rockefeller, in the November election.

Many political observers believed that with a Democrat in the White House, Jordan would be offered a cabinet post, an ambassadorship, or even a seat on the Supreme Court. Jordan herself expressed interest in becoming attorney general. (This is the top law-enforcement position in the United States government.) The congressperson and Carter met

Barbara Jordan shakes hands with newly elected President Jimmy Carter.

after he was elected, but in the end, Jordan remained in Congress for a third term.

Perhaps this was why, a year later, Jordan made a surprise announcement. She was retiring from politics when her term ended in 1978 because her "internal compass" told her to "turn in a different direction."[17] Stunned observers wondered if she were bored, or perhaps even seriously ill, but Jordan said no. She simply said that politics had become "too all-consuming."[18] She would leave Washington, D.C., and return to her home state of Texas.

Jordan had accomplished much in her six years as a member of Congress. She wrote an amendment to the Law Enforcement Assistance Administration that required the use of federal funds in a nondiscriminatory way. She also sponsored an amendment that broadened the Voting Rights Act of 1965 to include poor voters as well as those who did not speak English. Another of her many accomplishments was sponsoring the Consumer Goods Pricing Act of 1975 to ensure fair prices on many items.

Many people found it difficult to believe Jordan was leaving office. This forty-two-year-old woman devoted many years to public service and still had so many more to give. Yet Jordan was adamant: She was stepping out of the spotlight. She would still continue to contribute to American society, however. Jordan would become a college professor.

10

LIFE AFTER WASHINGTON, D.C.

"I never intended to become a run-of-the-mill person," Barbara Jordan once said.[1] Indeed, in the almost twenty years since she graduated from law school, Jordan proved she was anything but ordinary. She accumulated a number of impressive "firsts." Jordan was the first African-American woman elected to the Texas State Senate and the first African-American woman elected from the South to the United States Congress. She also was the first woman, and the first African American, to be keynote speaker at a political convention. In 1976, *Time* magazine selected her as one of its ten women of the year.

Barbara Jordan received an honorary degree from Harvard University in 1977. The following year, she would choose to leave public office.

Then, in 1978, Jordan voluntarily left public office. Political observers were curious. What was next for this remarkable woman? A year later, Jordan answered that question. She became a professor at the Lyndon B. Johnson School of Public Affairs at the University of Texas in Austin. She taught courses on policy development and on political values and ethics.

In the classroom, Jordan was a strict teacher. She assigned a lot of homework and expected her students to come to class thoroughly prepared to discuss the material. "She stands on formality—no, not formality, but politeness," one student said. "If you miss her class and don't apologize, you've committed two offenses of equal importance."[2]

Despite her toughness, Jordan proved to be a very popular professor. Her students called her B.J. and rushed to sign up for her classes. In fact, so many students wanted Professor Jordan that a lottery system was established. The winners received seats in her classroom, and the losers could try for a spot the following semester.

Jordan frequently entertained students at her ranch-style house near Austin. During these parties, the professor fired up the barbecue, played her guitar, and sang "Amazing Grace" and other favorite songs.

As she had during her days in Washington, D.C., Jordan tried to avoid publicity. Yet that did not stop members of the press from writing about her. They continued to speculate about the reasons behind her political retirement. Some publications noted that she weighed about fifty pounds less than when she was a congressperson and that she now needed a walker to get around. Sometimes she used a wheelchair. However, Jordan refused to provide details about her health.

Later, though, Jordan would speak more about why she left politics. She implied that all those "firsts" may have become too heavy a burden. "It's a heady experience for black elected officials, not easily handled," she said before fifteen hundred people at a dinner for the Joint Center for Political Studies in Washington, D.C. "It's shedding the mantle of the individual and taking on the robe of the entire race."[3]

She also hinted that she had become disillusioned with politics. For example, one time a student asked the professor why she had campaigned for President Carter in 1976 but not when he sought reelection in 1980. "I'm busy now," she replied. "I wasn't busy in 1976. I was serving in Congress."[4]

Also, Jordan told a magazine reporter that although she "did what I could" as a politician:

> . . . in Congress, one chips away, one does not make bold strokes. After six years, I had wearied of the little chips that I could put on a woodpile. And now that I am teaching, I think my future is in seeing to it that the next generation is ready to take over.[5]

In fact, whenever she was asked if she would attempt a political comeback, Jordan was firm. "No, I am not bitten anymore by the political bug," she said in 1983. "It takes a long time to become a good professor, and I intend to become a *very* good one."[6] She added that her contribution to society now would be to shape her students into "premier public servants who have a core of principles to guide them. They are my future, and the future of this country."[7]

Jordan insisted that she would not again hold office. Yet she did stay involved in the political world. From 1979 to 1981, she served on a board that advised President Carter on ambassador appointments. She also spoke out against Carter's successor, Ronald Reagan. Carter had proven to be an ineffective president, and the economy suffered under his leadership. Reagan, a former actor and California governor, soundly beat Carter when the president ran for reelection in 1980.

The new president increased defense spending and reduced taxes. He also eliminated many government programs. Jordan called Reagan's economic policies "a disaster for the poor."[8] She also said the president "has done a rather masterful job of presenting himself, his administration and his politics in a soft, glowing light. People don't see the stings or the pain."[9]

From 1979 to 1981, Barbara Jordan served on a board that advised President Jimmy Carter on ambassador appointments.

Jordan also became involved with Texans for Equal Justice. This group spoke out against Reagan's budget cuts in legal services for the poor. Another project was cofounding People for the American Way with television producer Norman Lear. The group stressed tolerance as well as freedom of expression. It was designed to balance the effects of the Moral Majority. That group, led by television evangelist Jerry Falwell, campaigned against abortion and homosexual rights and supported prayer in public schools.

In 1983 Jordan served on a panel that interviewed Democrats who wanted to run for president in 1984. Jordan made an exciting prediction. A woman would be on the Democratic ticket one day, she said. It could happen as early as 1988.[10]

Jordan's prediction came true—though much earlier than even she had anticipated. Walter Mondale, a former United States senator from Minnesota and Carter's vice president, became the Democratic presidential candidate in 1984. He chose as his running mate Geraldine Ferraro. The New York congressperson became the first woman to be nominated by a major political party to run for high office.

Democrats were hopeful, but the feeling was short-lived. In the November election, Mondale and Ferraro were beaten badly. Reagan and his running mate, George Bush of Texas, were reelected.

The same year as the Democrats' defeat, Jordan was named by *World Almanac* as one of the twenty-five most influential women in America. This was the tenth consecutive year she had received the honor. Jordan would receive acclaim elsewhere as well. During her career, she received almost thirty honorary doctorate degrees. They came from prestigious colleges and universities such as Harvard, Princeton, Notre Dame, William and Mary, Wake Forest, and Tuskegee. The former congressperson also was named Best Living Orator by the International Platform Association in 1984.

In 1987, Jordan returned to Washington, D.C. This time, she presented testimony to the Senate Judiciary Committee. Jordan spoke out against the nomination of Judge Robert Bork to the Supreme Court. She believed that he was too conservative and could make rulings that would adversely affect minorities. Jordan also was concerned about Bork's opposition to the Constitution's implied right to privacy.

Besides testifying against the judge, Jordan went on the television show *Meet the Press* to explain why she was against his nomination. Eventually, Bork was rejected. Instead, another nominee, Anthony Kennedy, became the new Supreme Court associate justice.

Another presidential election was scheduled for 1988. Reagan, who had been a popular president, was not allowed by the Constitution to run for a third term. His vice president, George Bush, became the Republican's choice for president. Dan Quayle of Indiana was his running mate.

The Democrats met in Atlanta, Georgia, in the summer of 1988 to choose their presidential candidate. They nominated Michael Dukakis, the governor of Massachusetts. Jordan delivered the speech seconding the nomination of Lloyd Bentsen as the vice presidential candidate. Bentsen was a senator from Jordan's home state of Texas. In the fall, the two candidates were defeated.

In August 1988, shortly after the convention, Jordan made headlines again. This time, though, it had nothing to do with politics. The former congressperson was found floating face down in the swimming pool at her home. She had been exercising when she went into cardiac arrest. Jordan was found by her female housemate and was revived by rescue workers. According to the doctor who treated her, the professor was very fortunate. She had come within "four to five minutes, ten minutes at most," of suffering severe brain damage or possibly even death.[11]

Jordan made a full recovery, but the episode again sparked many questions about her health. Many believed she had multiple sclerosis, a disease of the central nervous system. Characteristically, Jordan refused to divulge details. Eventually, though, she became unable to walk at all and used a wheelchair.

Yet Jordan's precarious health did not slow her down. She continued to teach at the University of Texas. She also served as a faculty adviser and helped recruit minority students to the university.

Then, in 1991, Jordan was appointed by Governor Ann Richards of Texas to be her "ethics guru." The normally press-shy Jordan consented to an interview with *Time* magazine. She explained to a reporter the duties of her job. "I question the Governor's proposed appointees about matters that are ethically sensitive," she said. "It's the things that are not blatant that get you into trouble."[12]

Jordan added that she was very concerned about the perceived lack of ethics in politicians. "I absolutely believe politics is an honorable profession," she said. "I believe only a very small percentage of people who are in public office are guilty of wrongdoing, of abusing their public trust."[13]

"It is so important for a public servant to sort out what is legal from what is ethical," she added. "I tell appointees, 'You must not engage in any fine-line drawing.'"[14]

Jordan also said that she offers advice to students thinking of pursuing political careers:

> I tell them, don't expect to get rich—the public does not pay its servants a great deal of money. Go do this

job because you want the government to run well and you think you can help it run well. And . . . if ever you decide you want to get rich then get out of government, because if you don't, I'll visit you in jail.[15]

Throughout the 1980s, Jordan had been disappointed by the men who had served in the nation's highest office. She believed that decisions they made had weakened civil rights. Now, with the 1992 presidential election looming, the economy was faltering. President Bush appeared to have little interest in domestic affairs.

Yet Jordan also recognized that the Democrats needed to reassess themselves. Strong leadership in that party had been lacking as well.

And so on July 13, 1992, Professor Jordan returned to Madison Square Garden in New York City. She was one of the keynote speakers of the Democratic National Convention. It was a duty she had performed sixteen years earlier at the same event in the same place. This time her speech was titled "Change." Jordan said:

There appears to be a general apprehension about the future which undermines our confidence. The American idea that tomorrow will be better than today has become destabilized by a stubborn, sluggish economy. . . . Public policy makers are held in low regard. Mistrust abounds.[16]

She continued:

We are not strangers to change. We calmed the national unrest in the wake of the Watergate abuses and we, the Democratic party, can seize this moment. We know what needs to be done and how to do it.[17]

She declared:

The American dream is not dead. True, it is gasping for breath, but it is not dead. However, there is no time to waste because the American Dream is slipping away from too many. It is slipping away from too many black and brown mothers and their children; from the homeless of every color and sex; from the immigrants living in communities without water and sewer systems. . . . We must profoundly change from the . . . environment of the Eighties, characterized by greed [and] selfishness . . . to one characterized by devotion to the public interest and tolerance. And yes, love.[18]

The speech was vintage Jordan, powerful and riveting. "Barbara Jordan used her time to tell Democrats something they needed to hear," declared *The Wall Street Journal* in an editorial. "If it doesn't work out for the Democrats in November, none of them should act confused. On Monday night, like it or not, they got it—with clarity and with eloquence."[19]

The Democrats did "get it." By the time the convention concluded, Arkansas governor Bill Clinton was the Democrats' choice for president. Tennessee senator Albert Gore, Jr., was his running mate. The two "baby-boomers," both in their forties, adopted the call for change and made it central to their election platform.

11

THE PRESIDENTIAL MEDAL OF FREEDOM

fter addressing the Democrats in July 1992, Jordan returned to her teaching job at the University of Texas. She watched with interest as Bill Clinton, the Democratic candidate for president, adopted the call for change while campaigning for the nation's highest office. Jordan had declared in her speech:

> We [Democrats] have been the instrument of change in policies which impact education, human rights, civil rights, economic and social opportunity, and the environment. These are policies firmly imbedded in

the soul of our party. We will do nothing to erode our essence. However, some things need to change. The Democratic Party is alive and well. It will change in order to faithfully serve the president and the future.[1]

Clinton went on to win the November election. He became the nation's forty-second commander-in-chief and the first Democrat to hold the office in sixteen years. In 1993, he turned to Jordan to help him enact some of the changes they both sought. The new president asked Jordan to lead the United States Commission on Immigration Reform.

Previously, Jordan had compiled even more honors to add to her long list. The main post office in Houston was dedicated to her in 1985. In 1986, she was named one of the twenty-five most influential women in America by *World Almanac*—for the twelfth consecutive year.

Four years later, in August 1990, Jordan was inducted into the National Women's Hall of Fame. She joined tennis player Billie Jean King, medical researcher Florence Siebert, and photojournalist Margaret Bourke-White as nominees for that year. More than forty women have been inducted into the Hall of Fame since it was established in 1968.

Jordan also had teamed with actor Tom Selleck and others in 1993 to form the Character Counts Coalition. This group sought to teach the nation's youth about trustworthiness, respect, responsibility, fairness, caring, and citizenship.

Now Jordan faced a new challenge. She accepted Clinton's assignment to lead the immigration panel. "I thought maybe I could have an impact," she said.[2] Jordan and her nine-member committee investigated problems that were caused by the huge number of people from other countries seeking to call America home. During the 1980s, the United States admitted more than 7 million legal immigrants. In 1994 alone, more than nine hundred thousand legal immigrants settled in the United States.[3] Many people believed these new immigrants put a strain on the nation's health-care and welfare systems and took jobs away from those who were already citizens.

Jordan's panel also looked at ways to stop illegal immigrants from entering the country. Studies have shown that as many as three hundred thousand people come to America illegally every year.[4] "In five years, this went from an issue in the corner to an unattractive mess in the middle of the table," said Frank Sharry, director of the National Immigration Forum, an advocacy group. "It has caused divisions, hatred, hostility, and extremism on both sides."[5]

Jordan and her committee conducted hearings. They also made recommendations to the president. One idea that received a lot of publicity was to create a national computer database of legal residents.

Employers would be able to call the database directly to verify that job applicants were legal citizens.

Some people criticized the proposal. They believed it would lead to government interference in private lives. Jordan argued that any negatives were outweighed by the benefits. She noted that under the present system, illegal immigrants simply presented easily forged documents to employers in order to land jobs. "Concerned about inadvertently hiring an illegal alien, employers discriminate against foreign-looking and -sounding citizens and legal immigrants," she said.[6]

"All employees must already provide a Social Security number," Jordan explained. "All that would be added is a requirement that employers call the computer registry to verify that the number is valid and was issued to someone authorized to work in the United States."[7]

Clinton did not act on Jordan's recommendation immediately. In August 1994, however, the president recognized her latest service to the country. He awarded the African-American woman the Presidential Medal of Freedom. This is the highest civilian award in the nation. As of 1995, only 144 Americans had received this prestigious honor for public service.

Jordan accepted her medal at a White House ceremony. "I have spent my career protecting the constitutional and civil rights of Americans," she told a reporter on the eve of the ceremony. "If I were in public office today, my primary task would be one of educating, communication, and pulling in those people who continue to feel so left out."[8]

She added, "There are many people who do not have the kind of material wealth which enables them to stand tall and productive. There are people who have not gotten the opportunity to earn and learn, which was the creed when I was growing up."[9]

The medal was satisfying recognition for Jordan's long and esteemed career. Yet this amazing woman by no means saw this as her final achievement. Despite ill health, Barbara Jordan had no plans to retire from a life of service. No doubt she planned to continue to follow some advice that her beloved Grandfather Patten gave her. "Just remember, the world is not a playground, but a schoolroom," he said. "Life is not a holiday, but an education. One eternal lesson for us all: to teach us how better we should love."[10]

In the 1990s, Jordan continued to teach at the University of Texas's Lyndon B. Johnson School of Public Affairs. She served on several corporate boards and was involved in civic and public-policy projects. She was all too aware that some of the changes she sought had not been realized. For example, Jordan supported the Equal Rights Amendment. She also wanted to see "some resolution and compromise" on

Barbara Jordan enjoyed her teaching position at the University of Texas. She is shown here in the early 1990s, teaching a class.

abortion.[11] The pro-choice advocate believed that the issue had become too divisive.

Moreover, some of the changes Jordan saw surely disappointed her. In June 1995, the Supreme Court ruled that election districts drawn up for racial purposes are likely to be unconstitutional. This is because race cannot be the main reason legislatures place voters within a particular district.[12] It was just such a redistricting that propelled lawyer Jordan to her first elected office. A similar redistricting led to her historic congressional victory.

The child of segregation continued to worry that America would struggle to achieve full racial equality. "But we must never stop trying," Jordan said. "We have come a long way, and we will go a lot further."[13]

Jordan also was confident that one day race would not be an issue. "I believe that there will be a black person one day who will run for president of the United States and be elected," she said.[14] "I don't know that I will see it in my lifetime," she added, "but I believe it will happen."[15]

Sadly, it did not happen while Jordan was alive. On January 17, 1996, Barbara Jordan died in her home state of Texas. She was fifty-nine years old. The cause of death was viral pneumonia as a complication of leukemia.[16]

"I feel a stabbing sense of loss at the passing of a good friend," said Lady Bird Johnson.[17] Mrs. Johnson

Barbara Jordan was a role model and a hero. This sketch of Jordan appeared on a brochure for the Capital Complex Visitor Center in Texas in 1995.

is the widow of the former president who had played such an important role in Jordan's political life.

Texas Governor George W. Bush, son of the former president, said, "Texas has lost a powerful voice of conscience and integrity. Barbara Jordan was a champion of our freedom, Constitution, and laws."[18]

President Clinton also expressed his sadness, saying that Jordan "challenged us as a nation to confront our weaknesses and live peacefully together as equals."[19]

When Jordan was still alive, she had expressed the hope that her deeds would continue to inspire long after her death. "I believe . . . that I have a spirit that is not going to disappear," she said. "That my body will die and disintegrate, but there is that basic law of physics, that matter is neither created nor destroyed.[20]

"Now the skin and bones will go back to dust," she continued. "But the spirit of that individual . . . will live. And in my view of religion . . . it is that spirit of Barbara Jordan that will continue to live.[21]

"In what state, in what sense, I don't know," concluded this woman who became a role model as well as a hero in her short lifetime. "But I do believe that for those of us who have lived well and tried to do things in a Christian and thoughtful and loving way, there is a constructive role for that spirit that will remain after the flesh is gone."[22]

Long live the spirit of Barbara Jordan.

CHRONOLOGY

1936—Barbara Charline Jordan is born in Houston, Texas, on February 21.

1952—Graduates at age sixteen from the all-black Phillis Wheatley High School, where she is named Girl of the Year.

1954—Supreme Court rules in *Brown* v. *Board of Education of Topeka* that segregation in public schools deprives African Americans of equal education.

1956—Graduates from Texas Southern University.

1959—Graduates from Boston University Law School; passes both the Massachusetts and Texas bar exams and opens a law practice in her parents' home.

1960—Works as a volunteer in the Texas campaign to elect Democrat John F. Kennedy as president of the United States.

1962—Runs for Texas House of Representatives but is defeated badly.

1964—Makes second try for the Texas House of Representatives but is defeated; Congress passes Civil Rights Act, which bans segregation and guarantees equal employment.

1966—After Texas redistricting, runs for Texas Senate; wins May primary, assuring her election in November.

1967—Is sworn in as the first African-American state senator in Texas since 1883.

1968—Runs unopposed for a second term in the state senate.

1971—Barbara Jordan Day is declared in Houston.

1972—Becomes Governor for the Day in Texas; is first African-American woman from the South elected to the United States House of Representatives.

1973—Arrives in Washington, D.C., as a member of the House Judiciary Committee.

1974—House Judiciary Committee begins formal hearings on possible impeachment of President Nixon; Jordan delivers powerful speech in televised House hearings on impeachment; Nixon resigns; Jordan is reelected to second term in the House.

1976—Delivers keynote address at Democratic National Convention; is reelected to a third term in the House.

1978—Retires from Congress.

1979—Becomes a professor at the University of Texas, Austin.

1982—Named as University of Texas Lyndon B. Johnson Chair of National Policy.

1984—Is named Best Living Orator by the International Platform Association.

1988—Gives speech at Democratic National Convention for vice presidential candidate Lloyd Bentsen; almost drowns in her swimming pool; makes a complete recovery.

1990—Is inducted into the National Women's Hall of Fame.

1991—Is appointed Special Counsel for Ethics by Governor Ann Richards.

1992—Delivers keynote address at the Democratic National Convention.

1993—Jordan and others establish Character Counts Coalition; President Clinton asks Jordan to head the United States Commission on Immigration Reform.

1994—Is awarded Presidential Medal of Freedom.

1996—Barbara Charline Jordan dies on January 17 at the age of fifty-nine in her home state of Texas. Cause of death is viral pneumonia as a complication of leukemia. She also had multiple sclerosis.

CHAPTER NOTES

Chapter 1

1. Michele Kay, "Helping Others 'Stand Tall': Jordan, 8 Others to be Awarded Presidential Medal of Freedom Today," *The Atlanta Journal/The Atlanta Constitution*, August 8, 1994, p. 7A.

2. Barbara Jordan and Shelby Hearon, *Barbara Jordan: A Self-Portrait* (Garden City, N.Y.: Doubleday, 1979), p. 139.

3. Molly Ivins, "Bragging on Barbara Jordan, A Hero," *The Atlanta Journal/The Atlanta Constitution*, August 13, 1994, p. A16.

4. Daniel Henninger, "A Woman of Substance," *The Wall Street Journal*, July 15, 1992, p. A12.

5. Ibid.

6. William Raspberry, "Honor Thy FOGIES," *The Washington Post*, October 11, 1993, p. 31A.

7. Bryna J. Fireside, *Is There a Woman in the House . . . Or Senate?* (Morton Grove, Ill.: Albert Whitman, 1994), p. 73.

8. Jordan and Hearon, p. 268.

Chapter 2

1. "Jordan, Barbara C.," *Current Biography Yearbook 1993*, (New York: H.W. Wilson, 1993), p. 290.

2. Bryna J. Fireside, *Is There a Woman in the House . . . Or Senate?* (Morton Grove, Ill.: Albert Whitman, 1994), p. 67.

3. Barbara Jordan and Shelby Hearon, *Barbara Jordan: A Self-Portrait* (Garden City, N.Y.: Doubleday, 1979), p. 63.

4. "The Congresswoman," *Newsweek*, July 4, 1976, p. 70.

5. Jordan and Hearon, p. 31.

6. David E. Rosenbaum, "Black Woman Keynoter: Barbara Charline Jordan," *The New York Times*, July 13, 1976, p. A24.

7. Jordan and Hearon, p. 46.

8. *Current Biography Yearbook 1993*, p. 290.

9. Fireside, p. 68.

10. *Current Biography Yearbook 1993*, p. 290.

11. Irwin Ross, "Barbara Jordan—New Voice in Washington," *Reader's Digest*, February 1977, p. 151.

12. U.S. Census Bureau statistics.

13. "The Congresswoman," p. 70.

14. Ross, p. 150.

Chapter 3

1. Bryna J. Fireside, *Is There a Woman in the House . . . Or Senate?* (Morton Grove, Ill.: Albert Whitman, 1994), p. 71.

2. "The Congresswoman," *Newsweek*, July 4, 1976, p. 70.

Chapter 4

1. Barbara Jordan and Shelby Hearon, *Barbara Jordan: A Self-Portrait* (Garden City, N.Y.: Doubleday, 1979), p. 93.

2. "Jordan, Barbara C.," *Current Biography Yearbook 1993*, (New York: H.W. Wilson, 1993) p. 290.

3. "A Sight for the Eyes of Texas," *Newsweek*, May 22, 1972, p. 34.

4. "The Congresswoman," *Newsweek*, July 4, 1976, p. 70.

5. Ibid.

Chapter 5

1. Irwin Ross, "Barbara Jordan—New Voice in Washington," *Reader's Digest*, February 1977, p. 151.

2. Liz Carpenter, "Barbara Jordan Talks About Ethics, Optimism, And Hard Choices in Government," *Ms.*, April 1985, p. 112.

3. Barbara Jordan, "How I Got There," *Atlantic Monthly*, March 1975, p. 38.

4. Ibid.

5. Rose Blue and Corinne Naden, *Barbara Jordan: Politician* (New York: Chelsea House, 1992), p. 51.

6. Jordan, p. 38.

7. E. D. Hirsch, Jr., Joseph F. Kett, and James Trefil, *The Dictionary of Cultural Literacy* (Boston: Houghton Mifflin, 1988), p. 268.

8. "Negroes Victors in Three Texas Races," *The New York Times*, May 9, 1966, p. A20.

9. "A Quiet Change," *Time*, May 20, 1966, p. 31.

10. Ibid.

11. Barbara Jordan and Shelby Hearon, *Barbara Jordan: A Self-Portrait* (Garden City, N.Y.: Doubleday, 1979), p. 132.

12. Ross, p. 151.

13. "A Quiet Change," p. 31.

14. Jordan, p. 38–39.

Chapter 6

1. Irwin Ross, "Barbara Jordan—New Voice in Washington," *Reader's Digest*, February 1977, p. 152.

2. Barbara Jordan, "How I Got There," *Atlantic Monthly*, March 1975, p. 39.

3. Ibid.

4. Molly Ivins, "Bragging on Barbara Jordan, A Hero," *The Atlanta Journal/The Atlanta Constitution*, August 13, 1994, p. A16.

5. "Comet in Congress: Barbara Jordan's Star Reaches Dizzy Heights for House Sophomore," *The Wall Street Journal*, February 6, 1975, p. A1.

6. Charles Sanders, "Barbara Jordan: Texan Is a New Power on Capitol Hill," *Ebony*, February 1975, p. 140.

7. "Jordan, Barbara C.," *Current Biography Yearbook 1993*, (New York: H.W. Wilson, 1993) p. 291.

8. Rose Blue and Corinne Naden, *Barbara Jordan: Politician* (New York: Chelsea House, 1992), p. 75.

Chapter 7

1. "A Sight for the Eyes of Texas," *Newsweek*, May 22, 1972, p. 34.

2. Ibid.

3. Meg Greenfield, "The New Lone Star of Texas," *Newsweek*, March 3, 1975, p. 31.

4. "A Sight for the Eyes of Texas," p. 34.

5. Charles Sanders, "Barbara Jordan: Texan Is a New Power on Capitol Hill," *Ebony*, February 1975, p. 140.

6. "A Sight for the Eyes of Texas," p. 34.

Chapter 8

1. B. J. Phillips, "Recognizing the Gentleladies of the Judiciary Committee," *Ms.*, November 1974, p. 72.

2. Ibid., p. 71.

3. Liz Carpenter, "Barbara Jordan Talks About Ethics, Optimism, And Hard Choices in Government," *Ms.*, April 1985, p. 76.

4. Phillips, p. 72.

5. David Rosenbaum, "Black Woman Keynoter: Barbara Charline Jordan," *The New York Times*, July 13, 1976, p. A24.

6. Phillips, p. 71.

7. "Jordan, Barbara C.," *Current Biography Yearbook 1993*, (New York: H.W. Wilson, 1993) p. 292.

8. Rosenbaum, p. A24.

9. Phillips, pp. 72–73.

10. The Staff of the Washington Post, *The Fall of a President* (New York: Delacorte Press, 1974), p. 195.

11. Ibid., p. xi.

12. Ibid., pp. xi, xiii.

Chapter 9

1. "Comet in Congress: Barbara Jordan's Star Reaches Dizzy Heights for House Sophomore," *The Wall Street Journal*, February 6, 1975, p. A1.

2. Irwin Ross, "Barbara Jordan—New Voice in Washington," *Reader's Digest*, February 1977, p. 149.

3. Charles L. Sanders, "Barbara Jordan: Texan Is a New Power on Capitol Hill," *Ebony*, February 1975, p. 141.

4. Ross, p. 150.

5. "Comet in Congress," p. A23.

6. Ibid.

7. Ibid.

8. Ibid., p. A1.

9. Ibid., p. A23.

10. Hope Chamberlin, *A Minority of Members: Women in the U.S. Congress* (New York: Praeger, 1973), p. 354.

11. "Barbara Jordan—Rising Political Star," *U.S. News and World Report*, February 9, 1976, p. 43.

12. Ibid.

13. Barbara Jordan, "Democratic Convention Keynote Address; Who Then Will Speak for the Common Good?" *Vital Speeches of the Day*, August 15, 1976, p. 645.

14. Ibid., p. 646.

15. "Jordan Is Immune to the Political Bug," *Newsweek*, December 19, 1983, p. 17.

16. "Barbara Jordan's Vision of America," *Ebony*, September 1976, p. 150.

17. "Update: Barbara Jordan, College Teacher," *Newsweek*, August 3, 1981, p. 5.

18. "Jordan Is Immune to the Political Bug," p. 17.

Chapter 10

1. David Rosenbaum, "Black Woman Keynoter: Barbara Charline Jordan," *The New York Times*, July 13, 1976, p. A25.

2. "Update: Barbara Jordan, College Teacher," *Newsweek*, August 3, 1981, p. 5.

3. "Jordan Reflects on Black Political Leadership at a Recent 'Joint Center' Fete," *Jet*, March 19, 1984, pp. 6–7.

4. "Update: Barbara Jordan, College Teacher," p. 5.

5. Liz Carpenter, "Barbara Jordan Talks About Ethics, Optimism, And Hard Choices in Government," *Ms.*, April 1985, p. 76.

6. "Jordan Is Immune to the Political Bug," *Newsweek*, December 19, 1983, p. 17.

7. Ibid.

8. "Jordan Reflects on Black Political Leadership," pp. 6–7.

9. "Jordan Is Immune to the Political Bug," p. 17.

10. Ibid.

11. "Barbara Jordan 'Better' After Swimming Accident," *Jet*, August 15, 1988, p. 4.

12. Bonnie Angelo, "An Ethical Guru Monitors Morality," *Time*, June 3, 1991, p. 9.

13. Ibid.

14. Ibid.

15. Ibid., p. 10.

16. Barbara Jordan, "Change: From What to What?" *Vital Speeches of the Day*, August 15, 1992, p. 651.

17. Ibid.

18. Ibid.

19. Daniel Henninger, "A Woman of Substance," *The Wall Street Journal*, July 15, 1992, p. A12.

Chapter 11

1. Barbara Jordan, "Change: From What to What?" *Vital Speeches of the Day*, August 15, 1992, p. 651.

2. Michele Kay, "Helping Others 'Stand Tall': Jordan, 8 Others to be Awarded Presidential Medal of Freedom Today," *The Atlanta Journal/The Atlanta Constitution*, August 8, 1994, p. A7.

3. Gil Klein, Media General News Service, "Immigrant Wave Hits 'Restrictionist Tide,'" *Richmond Times-Dispatch*, January 3, 1995, p. A1.

4. Ibid.

5. Ibid., p. A6.

6. Gil Klein, Media General News Service, "ID System: Debate Gets Louder," *Richmond Times-Dispatch*, January 5, 1995, p. A2.

7. Ibid.

8. Kay, p. A7.

9. Ibid.

10. Crystal Sasse Ragsdale, exhibit curator, program for "Barbara Jordan: Freedom Medalist and Texas Treasure," exhibit at the Capital Complex Visitors Center, Austin, Texas, January 12, 1995, through June 19, 1995.

11. Liz Carpenter, "Barbara Jordan Talks About Ethics, Optimism, And Hard Choices in Government," *Ms.*, April 1985, p. 112.

12. From wire reports, "Day of Judgment: 5–4 Decision Casts Doubt on Districts Based on Race," *Richmond Times-Dispatch*, June 30, 1995, p. A1.

13. "Barbara Jordan—Rising Political Star," *U.S. News and World Report*, February 9, 1976, p. 43.

14. Carpenter, p. 112.

15. Ibid.

16. Francis X. Clines, "Barbara Jordan Dies at 59; Her Voice Stirred the Nation," *The New York Times*, January 18, 1996, p. A1.

17. Ibid., p. B10.

18. The Associated Press, "Trailblazing Former Lawmaker Dies," *Richmond Times-Dispatch*, January 18, 1996, p. B3.

19. Ibid.

20. Carpenter, p. 112.

21. Ibid.

22. Ibid.

FURTHER READING

Angelo, Bonnie. "An Ethical Guru Monitors Morality." *Time*, June 3, 1991, pp. 10–11.

Carpenter, Liz. "Barbara Jordan Talks About Ethics, Optimism, and Hard Choices in Government." *Ms.*, April 1985, pp. 75–76, 112.

Chamberlin, Hope. *A Minority of Members: Women in the U.S. Congress.* New York: Praeger, 1973.

"Comet in Congress: Barbara Jordan's Star Reaches Dizzy Heights for House Sophomore." *The Wall Street Journal*, February 6, 1975, A-1.

Fireside, Bryna J. *Is There A Woman in the House . . . or Senate?* Morton Grove, Ill.: Albert Whitman, 1994.

Jordan, Barbara, and Shelby Hearon. *Barbara Jordan: A Self-Portrait.* Garden City, N.Y.: Doubleday, 1979.

Jordan, Barbara. "Change: From What to What?" *Vital Speeches of the Day*, August 15, 1992, pp. 651–652.

———. "How I Got There." *Atlantic Monthly*, March 1975, pp. 38–39.

———. "Who Then Will Speak for the Common Good?" *Vital Speeches of the Day*, August 15, 1976, pp. 645–646.

Kronenwetter, Michael. *The Congress of the United States.* Springfield, N.J.: Enslow Publishers, 1996.

Phillips, B. J. "Recognizing the Gentleladies of the Judiciary Committee." *Ms.*, November 1974, pp. 70–74.

Ross, Irwin. "Barbara Jordan—New Voice in Washington." *Reader's Digest*, February 1977, pp. 148–152.

Sanders, Charles L. "Barbara Jordan: Texan Is a New Power on Capitol Hill." *Ebony*, February 1975, pp. 136–142.

INDEX